MAY 2017

SandCastle

Rhyme Time

The Yaks Relax

Tracy Kompelien

Consulting Editor, Diane Craig, M.A./Reading Specialist

ABDO
Publishing Company

Published by ABDO Publishing Company, 4940 Viking Drive, Edina, Minnesota 55435.

Printed in the United States.

Credits
Edited by: Pam Price
Curriculum Coordinator: Nancy Tuminelly
Cover and Interior Design and Production: Mighty Media
Photo and Illustration Credits: BananaStock Ltd., Brand X Pictures, Corbis Images, Corel, Digital Vision, Hemera, Image 100, ImageState, Tracy Kompelien, PhotoDisc

Library of Congress Cataloging-in-Publication Data

Kompelien, Tracy, 1975-
    The yaks relax / Tracy Kompelien.
        p. cm. -- (Rhyme time)
    Includes index.
    ISBN 1-59197-821-1 (hardcover)
    ISBN 1-59197-927-7 (paperback)
    1. English language--Rhyme--Juvenile literature. I. Title. II. Rhyme time (ABDO Publishing Company)

    PE1517.K666 2004
    428.1'3--dc22
                                                2004050791

SandCastle™ books are created by a professional team of educators, reading specialists, and content developers around five essential components that include phonemic awareness, phonics, vocabulary, text comprehension, and fluency. All books are written, reviewed, and leveled for guided reading, early intervention reading, and Accelerated Reader® programs and designed for use in shared, guided, and independent reading and writing activities to support a balanced approach to literacy instruction.

Let Us Know

After reading the book, SandCastle would like you to tell us your stories about reading. What is your favorite page? Was there something hard that you needed help with? Share the ups and downs of learning to read. We want to hear from you! To get posted on the ABDO Publishing Company Web site, send us e-mail at:

sandcastle@abdopub.com

SandCastle Level: Transitional

Words that rhyme do not have to be spelled the same. These words rhyme with each other:

ax

snacks

backs

stacks

packs

tracks

relax

wax

sax

yaks

The Carsons chop wood with an ax.

Cam and Maria lie on their backs in the grass.

Painting pictures is Stephanie's favorite way to **relax**.

Caroline, Johnny, Tory, and Chad carry their homework in their **packs**.

Bill likes to make music.

He plays his toy **sax**.

Dylan and Julian eat frozen snacks.

Kaylee blew out the candles before the wax dripped onto the cake.

Brooke and Mason pile their blocks in short **stacks**.

Farmers in Tibet use **yaks** to pull plows and other heavy things.

Evan and Lily's skis leave long, skinny tracks.

The Yaks Relax

"What a busy week!" said the yaks.
"It is finally time to find a place to relax."

They closed the office
and turned off the fax.

Then they packed a few snacks.

They stuffed turkey dinners into sacks.

The yaks also packed a sax
and some candles made of wax.

They put the sacks
on their backs
and looked for a
good place to relax.

The yaks made tracks
until they reached some haystacks.

Off came the sacks
from their backs.

And the yaks began to relax.

Rhyming Riddle

What do you call piles of hatchets?

Ax stacks

Glossary

ax. a cutting tool with a long handle and a sharp blade

fax. a machine that scans documents and sends them over telephone lines to other fax machines

hatchet. an ax with a short handle that can be used with one hand

pack. short for backpack, a bag you wear on your back

sax. short for saxophone, a woodwind instrument that is made of metal

yak. a large, long-haired ox from Tibet and the mountains of central Asia

About SandCastle™

A professional team of educators, reading specialists, and content developers created the SandCastle™ series to support young readers as they develop reading skills and strategies and increase their general knowledge. The SandCastle™ series has four levels that correspond to early literacy development in young children. The levels are provided to help teachers and parents select the appropriate books for young readers.

Emerging Readers
(no flags)

Beginning Readers
(1 flag)

Transitional Readers
(2 flags)

Fluent Readers
(3 flags)

These levels are meant only as a guide. All levels are subject to change.

To see a complete list of SandCastle™ books and other nonfiction titles from ABDO Publishing Company, visit www.abdopub.com or contact us at:
4940 Viking Drive, Edina, Minnesota 55435 • 1-800-800-1312 • fax: 1-952-831-1632